HISTORICAL DEVELOPMENT OF THE NATIONAL MUSEUM OF BHUTAN

HISTORICAL DEVELOPMENT OF THE NATIONAL MUSEUM OF BHUTAN

DR. C.T. DORJI

FOREWORD BY
H.E. LYONPO DAGO TSHERING

PROMINENT PUBLISHERS
DELHI

First Edition 2004

HISTORICAL DEVELOPMENT OF THE NATIONAL MUSEUM OF BHUTAN

ISBN 81-86239-17-0

Published by Mrs. Tandin Dolma, Paro, Bhutan in collaboration with Prominent Publishers, 18 Vigyan Lok, Vikas Marg Extension, Delhi-110092, India (Phone 22150526, 22158906; Fax:011-22140454;E-mail: vipinm48@hotmail.com)

Distributor :

Chengay Dorji
Ta-Dzong. Paro, Bhutan
Phone: 975-8-272046

Printed at Print Line, New Delhi

Foreword

I know Dr. C.T. Dorji for a long time. He has brought out several publications on Bhutan's history, culture and even on the historical background of the road transport system in the Kingdom. All his works are very informative to casual as well as to serious readers.

The present compilation is a collection of his notes on the activities of the Ta-Dzong Museum in Paro from 1968 to 2002. It gives a good background to the historical development of the National Museum at the Ta-Dzong in Paro. I have read the first draft and he has decided to publish it in the present form. It is made more interesting and lively by the addition of several photographs. I am sure all readers on the Kingdom of Bhutan will find it useful.

(Dago Tshering)

CONTENTS

PREFACE

The book entitled "Historical Development of the National Museum of Bhutan" is based on my research papers prepared on different aspects of museology, archaeology, Buddhism, Bhutanese history and culture during last seven years at the National Museum of Bhutan. I have decided to put all the papers together and publish in the form of a book to enrich literature on the National Museum of Bhutan. Not only the subjects like museology, archaeology and conservation but the museum education is a new concept in our part of the world and this book is expected to throw some light on these subjects especially for those who do not have access to a museum. As a matter of fact, museum is the only institution which can keep Bhutanese rich cultural heritage alive for the benefit of future generations.

I must take this opportunity to thank all who have rendered helping hands to me in different forms. Among them, a special mention should be made of His Excellency Lyonpo Dago Tshering, the then Hon'ble Home Minister and Chairman, National Commission for Cultural Affairs, Royal Government of Bhutan without whose support I would not have come to the National Museum of Bhutan at Paro Ta-Dzong in October 1996 to put my knowledge of Bhutanese history and culture into practical use through organizing re-arranged special exhibitions in chronological sequence, conducting colloquia on Bhutanese history and culture and also preparing a preliminary draft of museum catalogue.

I should thank the Embassy of India in Bhutan and Indian Council for Cultural Relations (ICCR) for arranging my visit of a select museums and art galleries in India during May 1997 which has broadened my knowledge and understanding of the subjects. I am also thankful to the Nehru Trust, New Delhi for awarding 3-month UK Visiting Fellowship to me in 1999-2000 which gave me a special opportunity not only to visit the museums, art galleries and conservation centers in the UK but also interact with the museum authorities, curators and conservators.

I must thank Mrs. Tandin Dolma for her continuous support in my day-to-day works while writing this book. Moreover, I must thank her for publishing this book in collaboration with Mr. Surendar Mohan, Proprietor of Prominent Publishers, New Delhi.

Finally, my inexpressible thanks are due to His Excellency Lyonpo Dago Tshering, Ambassador of the Kingdom of Bhutan to India for graciously contributing a Foreword which has put life in this book.

Dr. C. T. Dorji

Paro Ta-Dzong
January 2003

I INTRODUCTION

Bhutan is a country nestled in the south-eastern Himalayan ranges bordered to the north by Tibetan Autonomous Region of China, to the east, west and south by Indian States of Sikkim, Arunachal Pradesh and Assam and West Bengal respectively completely land-locked and cut off by the mighty mountains. The country remained a sealed book for many centuries known as the world's last Shangri-La which inevitably led to the development of distinct languages and dialects, traditional culture, religious practices and preservation of its ecology and natural environments. Bhutan was opened to the outside world only four decades ago with the construction of motorable roads and introduction of motor vehicles with the initiative taken by the third hereditary King of Bhutan, Druk Gyalpo Jigme Dorji Wangchuck (r. 1952-72) who is considered as the chief architect and father of modern Bhutan. Bhutan is the only country in the world where the Vajrayana form of Mahayana Buddhism is retained as its religion today.

Bhutanese have treasured their natural environment as it is seen as a source of all life and the abode of the gods and spirits. Every mountain, hill, valley, rock, lake and even tree are considered as the dwelling place of gods, demi-gods and spirits and are not disturbed. Buddhism has been the predominant religion since the 7th century or earlier and has inculcated deeply the value that all forms of sentient beings, not just only human life, are precious and sacred. Given such a prevailing ethos which respects the natural environment, Bhutanese have lived in harmony for many centuries with nature and that the nation has its environment still pristine and intact today. Bhutan is rich in flora and fauna. Here the immense beauty of the Himalayas is contained in its diverse landscape with cascading rivers, conifer forests, rhododendron of different colours and blue poppies, long sweeping valleys, green fields of maize and paddy, imposing white-capped peaks. Its eco-system harbours some of the most exotic species of the south-eastern Himalayas with many species of birds and rhododendron, besides an astonishing variety of medicinal herbal plants and orchids. Spotting unusual and rare fauna in Bhutan is also almost obligatory. Golden languor, the species of long-tailed monkey and butterfly "Bhutan Glory" are unique to Bhutan. Yaks, snow leopard, Himalayan blue sheep and golden takin are ubiquitous on higher slopes of Bhutan. As a result, Bhutan has been identified as one of the 10 bio-diversity hot spots, as one of the 221 global endemic bird areas with an estimated 770 species of birds and over 50 species of rhododendron in the world.

Facts and figures of Bhutan are as follows:

a)	Area (sq. km.)	-	46500
b)	Districts (Dzongkhags)	-	20
c)	Blocks (Geogs)	-	201
d)	Population(1998)	-	638000
e)	Literacy rate (1998)	-	56%
f)	GDP (1998) - 16420		
g)	Forests & Agriculture (1995)		
	- Forest	-	72.5%
	- Pasture	-	3.9%
	- Agriculture	-	7.7%
	- Protected areas	-	26.23%
	- Others	-	15.9%
h)	All roads (1998)	-	3376 km.
i)	Tourists (1998)	-	6207

Bhutan's self-imposed isolation policy until early 60's kept the country outside the path of economic development in South Asia which prevented the country from fully benefiting from many of the medical, technical and scientific advances of the present day. On the other hand, it not only protected the country from many of the detrimental side effects of poorly planned or haphazard development of early 20 century, but also helped in religio-cultural development without external influence. While most of the Himalayan regions have seen the natural resources base severely compromised through deforestation, soil degradation, erosion and pollution, Bhutan's natural patrimony of extensive and varied forests, farmlands, pristine water and air remain largely intact without distortion and pollution. This is considered as blessing in disguise of the late economic development of the country. Nevertheless, during the second half of the 20th century, Bhutan has seen its isolation slowly and steadily eroded by the inexorable forces of modernization with the urbanization and introduction of Western education. Even if it wanted to, the country, no longer secluded, could not prevent itself from being swept up the surge of economic and social activity that is propelling the entire region into the 21st century. Bhutan now realized that it has much more to gain than to lose by joining in the march of progress but modernization is balanced with age-old traditional culture and value system.

I I DEFINITION OF MUSEUM

The word "Museum" means a building in which objects of historical, scientific, artistic, or cultural interest are stored and exhibited. Etymologically, the word "museum" is derived from Greek word *mouseion* meaning seat of the Muses or a university building. *Muse* is each of nine goddesses who preside over the arts and science in Greek and Roman mythology. It also means a woman or a force personified as woman who is the source of inspiration for a creative artist. The word *"muse"* when used as verb means to cogitate, meditate, think, dream, ponder, contemplate and deliberate. The human being, for more than thousand years, have created places where very special and valuable objects, artifacts and works of fine art provide milieu for *"musing"*

Early concept of museum especially that of archaeology was a ware-house of antiquity where precious and invaluable antique objects were stored and displayed to the visitors. Of course, people enjoyed these collections on display in the museums. However, now the concept of museum has changed from that of a ware-house of antiquities to an educational institution of cultural heritage, history, arts, science, design etc. The concept is further strengthened and developed by introduction of "museum education programme" and "mobile museum exhibition" which have been incorporated in the various activities of a museum. Every museum is now equipped with guide lecturers who are not only qualified in the subjects like history, culture, archaeology, art history and museology but also well trained to guide the visitors and give gallery talks. Museums are also equipped with reference library for research and publication, reading room, museum education programmes with good outreach. It is said that "a piece of drift wood or textile with profound background history is more precious and valuable than a piece of gold or diamond". Now the museum is a center of learning through visual display of the art objects which attract many visitors, teachers, students and research scholars.

The International Council of Museums (ICOM) which is an agency of the United Nations Educational Scientific and Cultural Organization (UNESCO) defines a museum as *"a non-profit making, permanent institution in the service of society and of its development, and open to the public, which acquires, conserves, researches, communicates and exhibits for the purposes of study, education and enjoyment, material evidence of man and his environment. (ICOM Statutes, 1974)".*

III PARO TA-DZONG BUILDING

The historic building of Paro Ta-Dzong which houses the National Museum of Bhutan was built in 1649 by the First governor of Paro valley, Ponlop Tenzin Drukda who later on became the 2nd Druk Desi (Temporal Head of Bhutan) and ruled the country from 1656 to 1658. It was built behind Paro Rinpung Dzong on a hillock as a watch-tower to safe-guard the main dzong from the Tibetan inroads. This peculiarly round seven storied building was constructed by Bhutanese architects using indigenous materials like stone, mud and wood which has two and a half meter thick walls withstood 354 years. It was converted into museum in 1968 because of its great historical significance. The building has also played an important role in the modern history of Bhutan. In 1872, Prince Ugyen Wangchuck, later on destined to become the first hereditary monarch of Bhutan, was sent by his father Tongsa Ponlop Jigme Namgyal to quell the insurrection by Paro Ponlop Tshewang Norbu. Prince Ugyen Wangchuck remained in Paro to sort out the political problems and put them in order. In the process, a plot was hatched to assassinate the young prince. However, the plot was discovered by his father and he was saved through negotiation in Ta-Dzong.

IV CONCEPT OF MUSEUM IN BHUTAN

It is said that "Rome has no museums but Rome itself was a museum". Similarly, Bhutan has no museums but Bhutan itself is a museum. The genesis of the museum movement in Bhutan can be traced back to the establishment of monasteries and temples beginning with the construction of Paro Kyichhu Lhakhang and Bumthang Jampal Lhakhang in the 7th century AD by the 33rd Buddhist King of Tibet, Srongtsan Gampo. These monasteries and temples served as museums in Bhutan because all art treasures, images made of precious metals, scriptures and paintings were preserved and conserved in them for worship, study and enjoyment. Since early concept of museum especially that of archaeology was a ware-house of antiquity where precious and invaluable antique objects were stored and displayed for worship and study, a Bhutanese word for museum was coined when the National Museum was established in 1968. Two Bhutanese words were joined together *"Namsay"* meaning God of wealth and *"Bangzyo"* meaning treasure house. The Bhutanese word *"Namsay Bangzyo"* means the treasure of the God of wealth or museum. Thus. *"Druk Gyalyong Namsay Bangzyo"* means the National Museum of Bhutan.

V AIMS, OBJECTIVES AND STRATEGY OF MUSEUM

The aims, objectives and strategy of the Museum are as follows:

(i) to acquire and display Bhutan's distinctive art and culture to the outside world, through exhibition in the National Museum at Paro Ta-Dzong as well as by organizing exhibitions outside the country;

(ii) to publicize about Bhutanese rich culture, tradition, religion, history and art;

(iii) to collect and preserve the cultural heritage of the country in its physical and non-physical forms for future research works.

(iv) to stop the illicit trafficking of the art objects to outside the country.

In order to achieve the above objectives, as a strategy, the National Museum has enriched and enlarged its collections with many art objects which were displayed in chronological sequence through re-arranged special exhibitions beginning 1996. The lighting systems have been improved and the objects were chemically treated by the trained conservators. The museum staff were trained in the fields of museology and conservation. Several exhibitions were organized to promote our rich cultural heritage outside the country.

VI INTRODUCTION AND DEVELOPMENT OF MUSEUM IN BHUTAN

The necessity to establish a National Museum was felt by late His Majesty, Druk Gyalpo Jigme Dorji Wangchuck (r. 1952-1972) in 1965 to conserve, preserve and promote rich Bhutanese cultural heritage. His Majesty commanded the Ministry of Development to renovate the historic 17th Century old building of Paro Ta-Dzong which was built by the First Governor of Paro Valley, Tenzin Drukda to house the National Museum. The 7 storied building was renovated by the then Ministry of Development in 1965 to 1968 and an approach motorable road was also constructed. The National Museum was opened to the public and visitors in 1968. Initially, it was under the administrative control of the Directorate of Education, Royal Government of Bhutan from 1965 to 1970. Then it was upgraded to a Department and remained under the administrative control of the Ministry of Finance from 1970 to 1985. When Special Commission for Cultural Affairs was established in 1985, the National Museum was also placed under its administrative control for preservation, conservation and promotion of Bhutanese culture, tradition and religion for the benefit of younger generation as well as foreign tourists.

Some of the finest art specimens, including master pieces of different metal sculpture and paintings of different periods and the pulsating life of Bhutan as expressed in objects of art created during her three thousand years of history were acquired, displayed and opened to the public in 1968. During the period 1974-1976 further major repair works were carried out, the electrification was improved and most of the galleries were opened to the public. In course of time, the show-cases were further improved and re-electrification was done in 2000 with the financial assistance from the Japanese Cultural Grant and all the galleries were opened to the public. The National Museum of Bhutan was the only multipurpose museum in the country till beginning of the 21st century. Now the Council of Ministers had decided to establish a museum in every dzongkhag beginning with the Textile Museum and Folk Heritage Museum at Thimphu which were inaugurated on 2 June 2001.

The Museum is an important institution of public education. We normally think of lectures or books whenever we talk of education. It is however, clear that neither books nor lectures can bring vividly before the public the understanding of the past glory. In a museum, history is revealed before us in stone and colour, for instance statues of Buddha and Bodhisattva bring vividly before us the grace and artistic beauty of Buddhist life and the high degree of culture evolved by the ancient people.

VII ADMINISTRATIVE STRUCTURE OF THE NATIONAL MUSEUM

The National Museum was established as a brain-child of His Majesty, Druk Gyalpo Jigme Dorji Wangchuck. As such, it received both administrative and financial support on top priority from all concerned authorities.

Initially the National Museum was as a section under the administrative control of the Directorate of Education, Ministry of Development. It was transferred to the Ministry of Finance, Royal Government in 1970 as a Department. However, when the National Commission for Cultural Affairs was established in 1985, the National Museum was placed under its administrative control as a full-fledged Department.

Administratively, the museum has four sections i.e.

(i) Administrative and Finance Section,
(ii) Curatorial and Display Section,
(iii) Conservation & Preservation Section,
(iv) Research and Publication Section and
(v) Audio-Visual & Filming Section

List of successive Chairman of National Commission of Cultural Affairs

(i) H. E. Lyonpo Tamzhi Jagar
(ii) H. E. Lyonpo Dago Tshering
(iii) H. E. Lyonpo Thinley Gyamtsho

List of successive Directors of the National Museum

(i)	Geshay Tshewang	1968 - 1973
(ii)	Mynak R. Tulku	1973 - 1999
(iii)	Sonam Topgay	1999 -

List of Museum staff as on 31 December 1996

(i)	Mynak R. Tulku	-	Director
(ii)	Dr. C. T. Dorji	-	Joint Director
(iii)	Chime Wangmo	-	Curator
(iv)	Dorji Namgyel	-	Asstt. Curator
(v)	Gem Tshering	-	Conservator
(vi)	Dorji Wangchuk	-	Lab. Assistant
(vii)	Deki Yangzom	-	LDC/Typing
(viii)	Sangchu	-	Museum Asstt.
(ix)	Sangay Wangdi	-	-do-
(x)	Mindu	-	-do-
(xi)	Kencho	-	-do-
(xii)	Four	-	Night Guards
NB	Total staff strength	-	15

List of Museum staff as on 31 December 2002

(i)	Sonam Topgay	-	Acting Director
(ii)	Dr. C. T. Dorji	-	Joint Director
(iii)	Khenpo Phuntsok Tashi	-	Researcher
(iv)	Dorji Namgyel	-	Asstt. Curator
(v)	Darick Dorji	-	Accountant
(vi)	Pema Choki	-	Comp. Operator
(vii)	Karma Phuntsho	-	Cameraman
(viii)	Gem Tshering	-	Conservator
(ix)	Dorji Wangchuk	-	Lab. Assistant
(x)	Deki Yangzom	-	Museum Asstt.
(xi)	Tenzin Phuntsho	-	Museum Asstt.
(xii)	Tandin Dhendup	-	Museum Asstt.
(xiii)	Mindu	-	Museum Asstt.
(xiv)	Kencho	-	Museum Asstt.
(xv)	Driver	-	One
(xvi)	Night Guards	-	Four
(xvii)	Sweeper	-	One
(xviii)	Gardener	-	One

NB Total staff strength - 21

The National Museum made a modest beginning to restructure and reinforce the museum staff by appointing and replacing appropriately qualified personnel in the curatorial section, conservation laboratory, research section and administration e.g. an Assistant Curator with M.A. in Buddhist Studies was transferred from Dratshang Lhentshog, Thimphu to the National Museum, Paro in July 1996 and a Joint Director with Ph.D. degree in Bhutanese history and culture was transferred from the Royal Institute of Management, Thimphu to the National Museum, Paro in October 1996. In July 1999, the National Commission for Cultural Affairs re-shuffled the Head of the Divisions under its administrative control and the Head of AFD/NCCA was transferred to the National Museum as its Acting Director. At the same time, a Researcher with M.A. in Buddhist Studies was also transferred from the National Library, Thimphu to the National Museum, Paro to look after the research and publication activities.

Recognizing the need and importance of trained manpower for the development of the National Museum, the Royal Civil Service Commission most graciously approved and recruited a Computer Operator, an Accountant, a Cameraman, 2 Conservators, a Film Editor, an Asstt. Curator, an Asstt. Research and Cataloguing Officer, 2 Drivers, a Gardener and a Sweeper.

The next important step for the National Museum now is to complete the restructuring and reinforcing exercise of the museum staff by appointing and replacing appropriately qualified personnel to discharge the job responsibilities more efficiently and effectively especially the Museum Assistants who are directly in touch with the visitors and dignitaries. The present Museum Assistants are uneducated and they cannot guide the visitors and explain the art objects on display. At the same time, there is shortage of Museum Assistants to cater to all galleries at 7 floors of Ta-Dzong Museum. As such, it is imperative on the part of the museum management to request the concerned authorities to appoint Museum Assistants possessing academic qualification at least Class X passed who are fluent in both Dzongkha and English. So that they could be trained to perform the duty of Museum Guides and explain the exhibits in the respective floors at Ta-Dzong Museum in addition to their job responsibility as Museum Assistants which is considered very important.

In view of the above facts, the National Museum has an inescapable need of following additional appropriately qualified and trained manpower to complete the restructuring and reinforcing exercise of the museum staff:

(i)	Chemist (B. Sc. Hon. in Chemistry)	-	1
(ii)	Museum Edn. Officer (B.Ed.)	-	1
(iii)	Lab. Assistant (Class XII passed with Sc.)	-	1
(iv)	Adm. Asstt. or Adm. Officer (Class X/Graduate)	-	1

VIII FINANCIAL RESOURCES OF THE NATIONAL MUSEUM

The National Museum as a full-fledged Department at par any other Department under different Ministries is funded by the Royal Government of Bhutan. Annual budget is proposed to the Ministry of Finance projecting both capital and current budget for the financial year. In addition to the RGOB funding, the National Museum also receives financial grant from the following donor agencies mainly for training, study tour, publications and equipment:

(i) UNESCO
(ii) Japan Foundation Asia Center
(iii) Japan Cultural Grant
(iv) Ford Foundation
(v) Smith Sonian

IX ACQUISITION POLICY AND COLLECTION OF ART OBJECTS

The National Museum collected all kinds of cultural properties, textiles and religious objects in the beginning since it is a multipurpose museum. Now it has restricted to acquire rare and valuable art objects, religious artifacts and master pieces for its collection. There is "Purchase Committee" of art objects constituted by 13 members chaired the Secretary, National Commission for Cultural Affairs and a Member-Secretary.

The museum's collection has been enriched and enlarged with additional acquisition of art objects as the National Museum has been receiving annually Nu. 0.8 m under the acquisition of art objects from the Department of Budget and Accounts, Ministry of Finance, RGOB. There are gaps in the present collections and it is necessary to fill up the gaps and add more objects of national importance.

X RECORD AND DOCUMENTATION

The National Museum has maintained a register for the art objects called "Thram" as per monastic system. All art objects after purchase or received from higher authorities are entered in the Thram and signed by the Director of Museum as well as Finance Minister or Finance Secretary when the National Museum was under the administrative control of the Ministry of Finance. When it was transferred to the National Commission for Cultural Affairs, the Director of Museum was authorized to sign the Thram on the basis of the approval obtained from the Chairman, National Commission for Cultural Affairs.

The theft and vandalism has endangered the ancient Bhutanese culture. The ancient arts and crafts have been fast loosing its ground or gravely threatened by the commercial outlook and cheap mechanical productions of today.

The proper recording and documentation of both new acquisitions and existing collections in the National Museum with appropriate standards and the internal rules and conventions of museum is most important professional responsibility. The documentation would provide accountability control over every item in the collection; accessibility to information and material at any time and accurately gives history and provenance of each object. The present maintenance of record in the museum is according to the monastic system, which is simple, unscientific, undescriptive. Many entries are casual and does not provide enough information about the objects.

Art Museum needs to store lots of data about the collections. Other than that, the need to be able to preserve information, track the collection and account for one's actions is important for any type of museum.

The documentation of artifacts in the museum would be the core activity which will include proper accession number, identification of the objects, title of the object, classification, how acquired (gift/purchase etc.), source, location, material, size, maker, date, description, association, value etc. With this, the size and complexity of the National Museum collection can be grasped very easily and where even a small staff can handle it.

XI GALLERIES AND DISPLAYS

Paro Ta-Dzong building has seven stories, out of which six stories have been renovated and converted into galleries to display various art objects in 1968. The average number of art objects on permanent display at Paro Ta-Dzong is around 1500 items. They were displayed subject-wise from 1968 to 1995 till re-arranged special exhibitions were planned to begin in 1996 based on the initiative taken by H. E. Lyonpo Dago Tshering, Hon'ble Home Minister and Chairman, National Commission for Cultural Affairs.

6th Floor:
- Tshogshing Lhakhang
- Gallery of Philately of Bhutan
- Photographs of all Dzongs and monasteries

5th Floor:
- Second re-arranged special exhibition on "Medieval Bhutan" (Part - I) covering period from 11 to 15 century AD
- Gallery of Thangka paintings
- Gallery of images with Namsay Phodrang in the center

4th Floor:
- First re-arranged special exhibition on "Dawn and Early History of Bhutan" covering period upto 10 century AD

- Third re-arranged special exhibition on "Medieval Bhutan" (Part - II) covering period from 15 to 16 century AD
- Ancient arms, ammunitions and armours of Bhutan as part of the 3rd exhibition

3rd Floor:
- Gallery of decorative arts including tea pots made of different metals like bronze, copper, silver, clay and other utensils
- Gallery of jewelry, costumes and other decorative arts
- Fourth special exhibition of Photographs covering 25 years of present His Majesty's coronation
- Fifth re-arranged special exhibition on "Zhabdrung Era" focused on the 17 century AD

2nd Floor:
- Gallery of religious artifacts, objects and costumes
- Gallery of natural history of Bhutan including wild animals, birds, reptiles and butterflies
- Gallery of lacquer-ware and wooden utensils of daily use

1st Floor:	-	Gallery of bamboo and cane products of daily use
Ground Floor-		Gallery of urns made of different metals and other utensils used in the olden days
	-	6th special exhibition on 18 and 19 century AD

The National Museum of Bhutan has good collection of Thangkas which are displayed in the Thangka gallery on the fifth floor divided into three sections. The first section of Thangkas arranged in chronological order to depict the origin of Buddhism. The Thangkas in the second section are arranged to describe the development of Buddhism in India especially by the 8 Buddhist Masters *(Zamling Gyendrug Chhognyi)*. The third section of thangkas explains the introduction and development of Buddhism in Bhutan from the 8th century AD onwards.

XII RE-ARRANGED SPECIAL EXHIBITIONS

The dawn of language is the dawn of mankind. The mankind in our part of the world has been enriched by the dawn in Buddhism. It is often said and written that Buddhism was the greatest civilizing influence in Asia. Wherever it has reached, it introduced not only the fine arts, pageantry and literature to the people but also taught the values of tolerance, non-violence and sense of brotherhood among all living beings. Buddhism and cultural heritage of Bhutan are intricately interlinked. It is in this spirit that the treasures or art objects of the National Museum have been reviewed and re-arranged to project the cultural heritage of Bhutan in proper perspective.

The treasures of the National Museum of Bhutan have been reviewed and re-arranged to project the cultural heritage of Bhutan in proper perspective beginning 1996 with the view that through such exercises and re-arranged special exhibitions in a chronological order, the significance of Bhutanese history and culture and Buddhism could be presented to the audience with greater clarity. It would not only show the artifacts as they developed through our history but also bring out the changes that have occurred as part of the changing needs of the society.

The first re-arranged special exhibition on "Dawn and Early History of Bhutan" covering period upto 10 century was opened in 1996 which include objects of the stone age (6000-8000 B.C.); archaeological remains of King Bangtsho Gyalpo (600-800 AD); some rare photographs of images and buildings (600-1100 AD); development of Dzongkha script and book of Prajna Paramita; replica of treasure stupa revealed by Terton Guru Chhowang (6th to 11th century AD); with photograph of original Stupa in the background and an ancient huge bell dating to the 7th century AD.

The second re-arranged special exhibition on "Medieval Bhutan" (Part - I) covering period from 11 to 15 century was opened in 1997. This gallery has 12th century bronze image of Lord Buddha blessed by Phajo Drugom Zhigpo; remains of iron chain from Tachhogang bridge (14th century AD) are some of the objects on display.

The third re-arranged special exhibition on "Medieval Bhutan" (Part - II) covering period from 15 to 16 century was opened in 1998. These three re-arranged special exhibitions displayed on the 4th floor are mostly artifacts available at the National Museum of Bhutan which include image of Guru Padmasambhava revealed by Terton Padma Lingpa and objects associated with Pha Dung Dung are some of the principle exhibits on medieval Bhutan.

The 4th special exhibition of 1999 was "Photo Exhibition" as part of the Silver Jubilee celebration of our present Majesty on 2 June 1999. The photographs include Royal Entourage within the country especially during Five Year Plan and Mid-term Review meetings, visit of hospitals and schools. Visit of the State guests to Bhutan and their interaction with His Majesty, Druk Gyalpo.

The 5th re-arranged special exhibition on "Zhabdrung Era" covered significant deeds of Zhabdrung Ngawang Namgyal was opened in 2000. The artifacts include the tooth relic of Zhabdrung Ngawang Namgyel's pet dog which accompanied him to Bhutan in 1616 AD, his great seal of Nga-Chudrug, thangkas of his previous life, Kuenkhen Padma Karpo; his father, Mipham Tenpi Nyima; his own thanks; the first Je Khenpo, Neten Pekar Jungney; the first Druk Desi, Umzey Tenzin Drugyel; his regent and the 4th Druk Desi, Gyalsay Tenzin Rubgye; photographs of 8 dzongs built during the reign of Zhabdrung Ngawang Namgyel; rank structure based upon monastic order e.g. orange coloured scarf for His Majesty, Druk Gyalpo and His Holiness, Je Khenpo; orange coloured scarf for the ministers and 4 Buddhist Masters *(Lopon Zhib)*; red coloured scarf for knighted officers and monks and white scarf with fringe for general public; 17th century old decorative arts like mithun horns, water-buffalo horns, small size urn *(throchung)* with 8 lucky signs *(Tashi-Dagay)* and 8 lucky signs oil lamp with wooden stand *(Lawang)* and consecration ceremony called *"Zhudrel Phuensum-tshogpa"*. The 4th and 5th special exhibitions are on permanent display on the 3rd floor.

The 6th re-arranged special exhibition on 18 to 19 century opened in May 2001 is also on permanent display on the ground floor of Paro a-Dzong. The objects include iron torch used in the warfare in the olden days, Bhutanese helmet *(Chabob)* made of silk and wire mash, iron, shield *(Dali)* made of rhinos hide, cane, Bhutanese sword *(Pata Hoshichem),* Bhutanese arrow *(Dha)* made of bamboo, feather and metal point; bow made of bamboo *(Zhu)* and Bhutanese quiver *(Sorey)* made of bamboo to keep arrows; Lash *(Sobi Teycha);* Battle flag*(Tsenda);* Bhutanese belt *(Kochhab)* is made of leather, silver and gold and used along with the sword; decorated Saddle *(Gah)* made of wood, copper, cloth, gold and leather; wooden Saddle *(Gah)* made of wood, copper, cloth, gold and leather; leather Saddle *(Gah)* made of leather; used by Bhutanese women in the olden days.

These exhibitions which remain as a part of the permanent display in the National Museum of Bhutan at Paro Ta-Dzong are expected to share our past glory vividly with the present and future generations. Nevertheless, there are many gaps which need to be filled in with relevant information and art objects in course of time which is a great challenge for the National Museum of Bhutan.

In addition to the above special exhibitions, the National Museum also sent exhibitions on Bhutan to USA, Europe, Japan and India.

Plate # 1

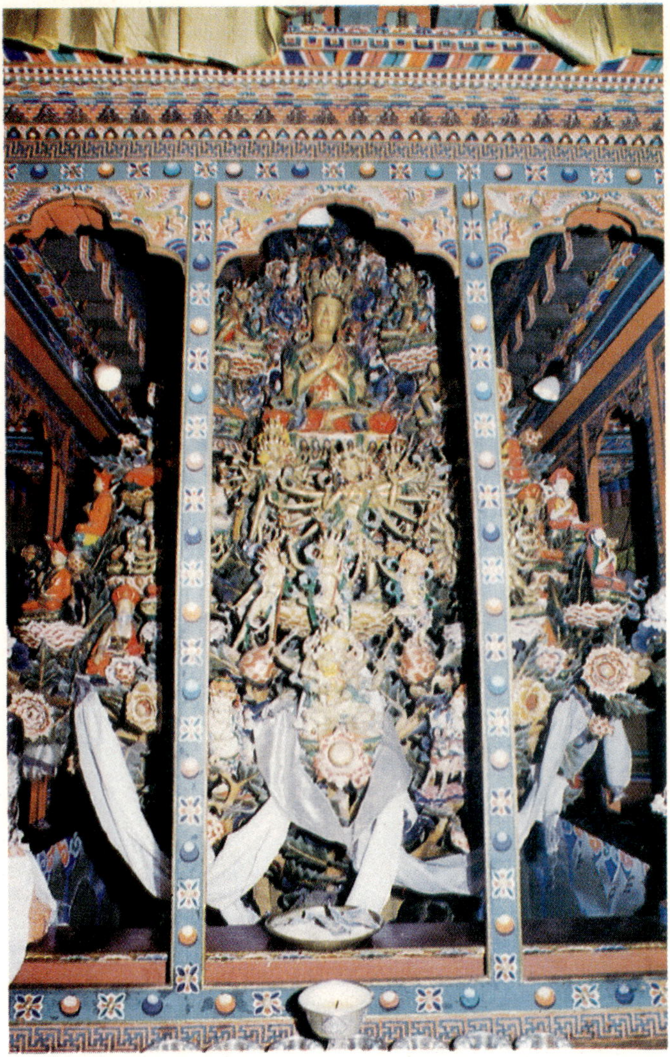

Sixth Floor: Tshogshing Lhakhang (Temple of Tree of Wisdom or Field of Buddhas). Eastern side depicting Buddha Vajra Dhara (RDORJE-CHHANG) in the centre top with Indian saint Tilopa and Naropa and Tibetan Master Marpa and Milarepa and other teachers of Kagyu lineage.

Plate # 2

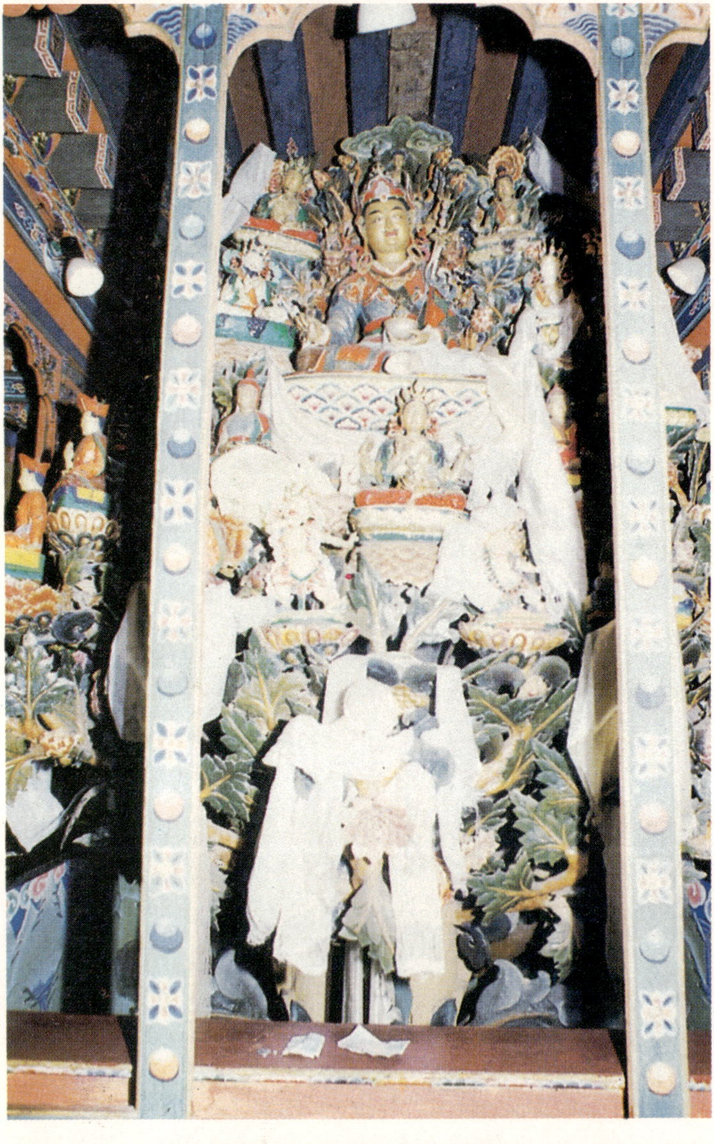

Sixth Floor: Tshogshing Lhakhang (Temple of Tree of Wisdom or Field of Buddhas). Western side depicting Guru Padmasambhava, the second Buddha who brought Buddhism to Bhutan in 747 AD

Plate # 3

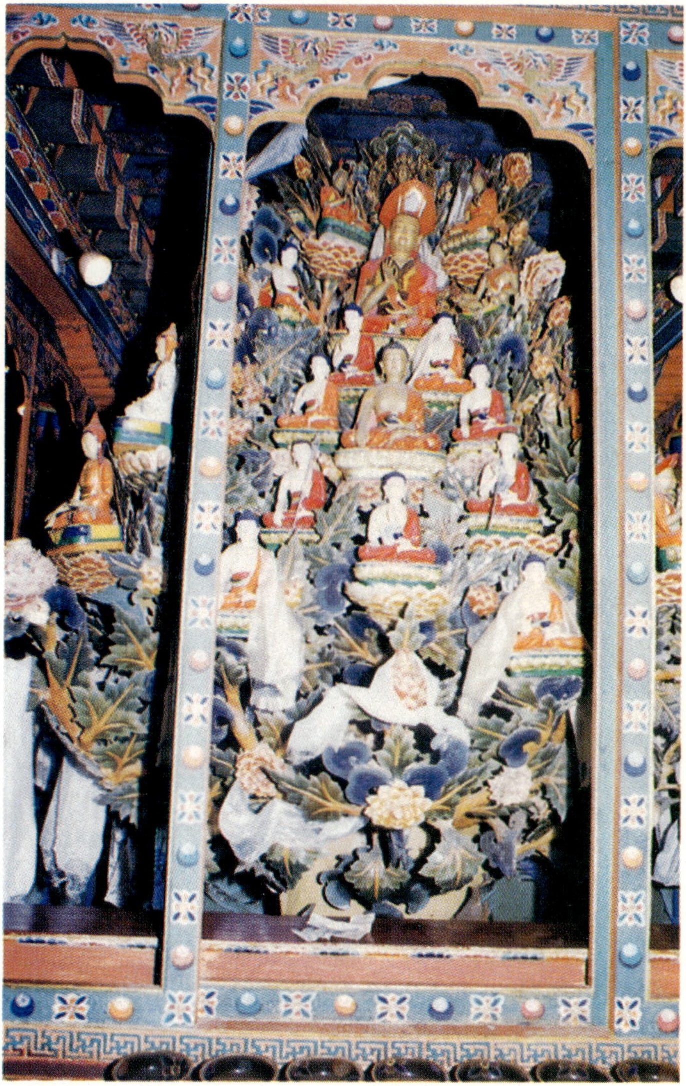

Sixth Floor: Tshogshing Lhakhang (Temple of Tree of Wisdom or Field of Buddhas). Southern side depicting Dagpo Lhaje in the centre top with Gautama Buddha flaned by two of his chief disciples - Shari Putra and Mahamongalayan

Plate # 4

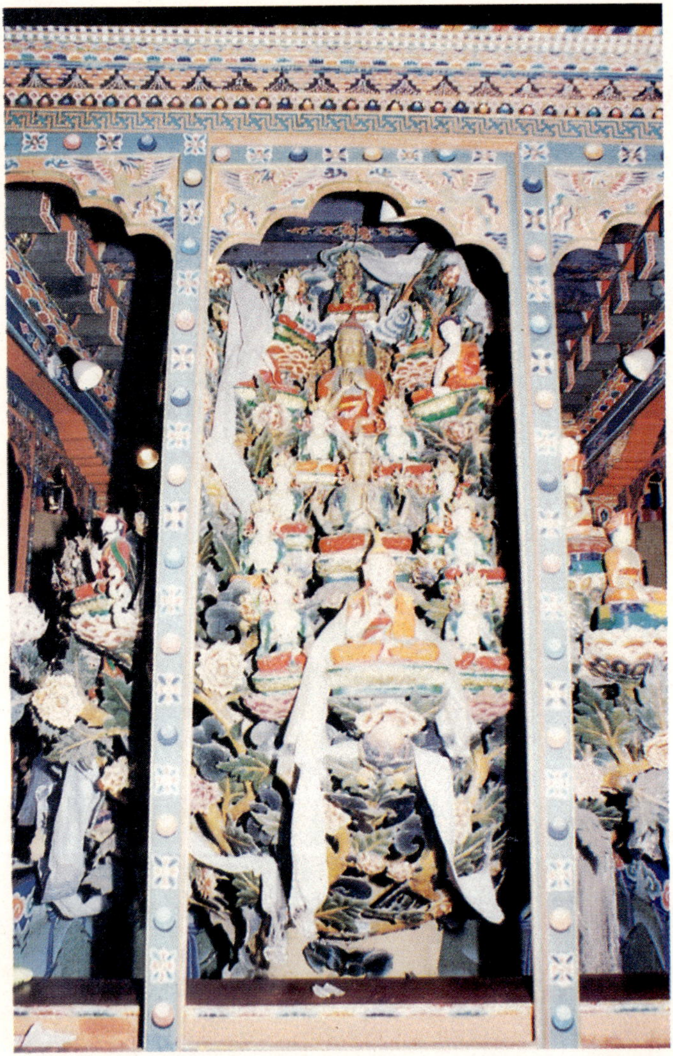

Sixth Floor: Tshogshing Lhakhang (Temple of Tree of Wisdom or Field of Buddhas). Northern side depicting Atisa Dipankara Srijna (Jowo Je Palden Atisha) of Bengal (Modern Bangladesh) in the centre top with Avalokiteshvara (Phagpa Chenrezi) and Eight Bodhisattvas (Ashta Upaputra)

Plate # 5

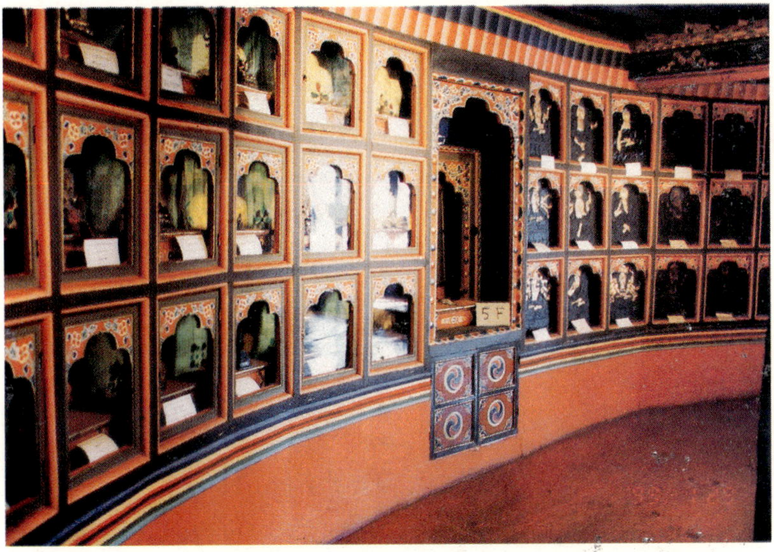

Fifth Floor: Statues made of bronze, copper, wood, ivory, rhinocero horn and slate carved figures of Buddhist saints, protecting deities, gods and goddesses

Plate # 6

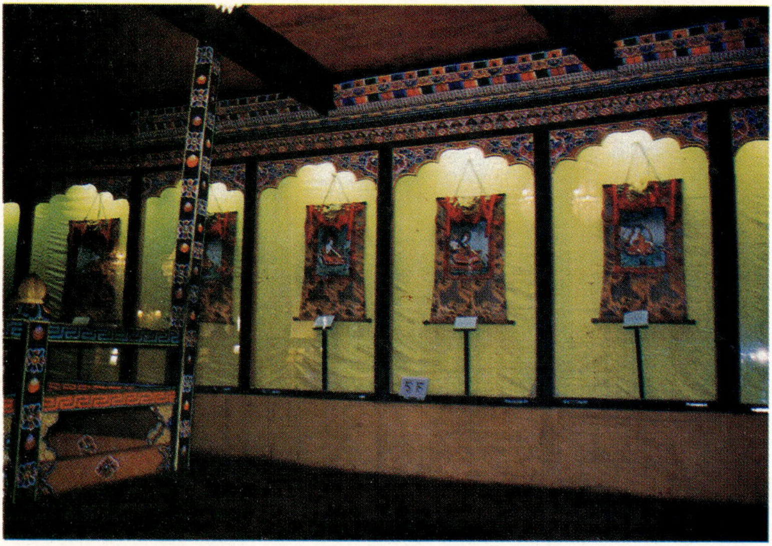

Fifth Floor: Gallery of Thangkas
(Religious paintings)

Plate # 7

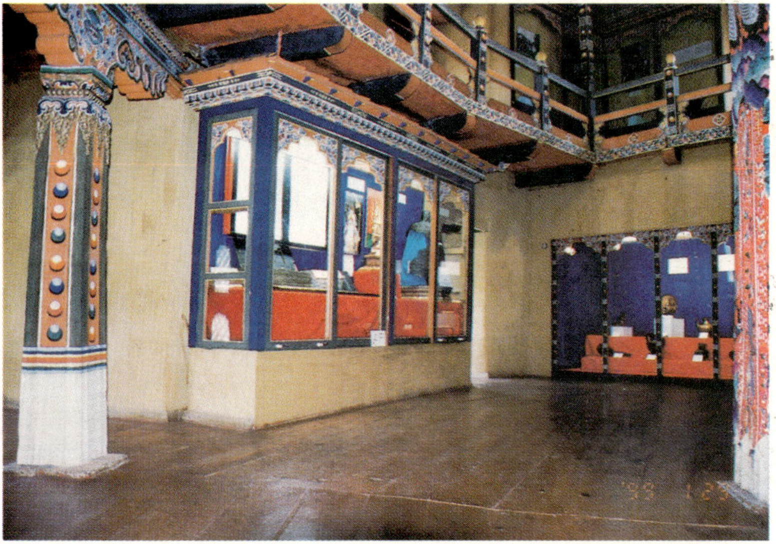

Fourth Floor: 1st rearranged special exhibition of 1996 on the theme of "Dawn and Early History of Bhutan" covering period upto 10 century AD

Plate # 8

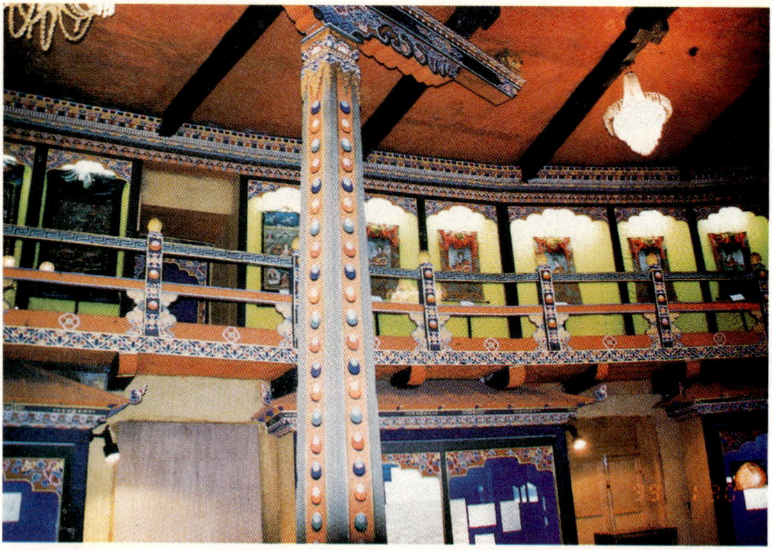

Fourth Floor: 1st rearranged special exhibition of 1996 on the theme of "Dawn and Early History of Bhutan" covering period upto 10 century AD

Plate # 9

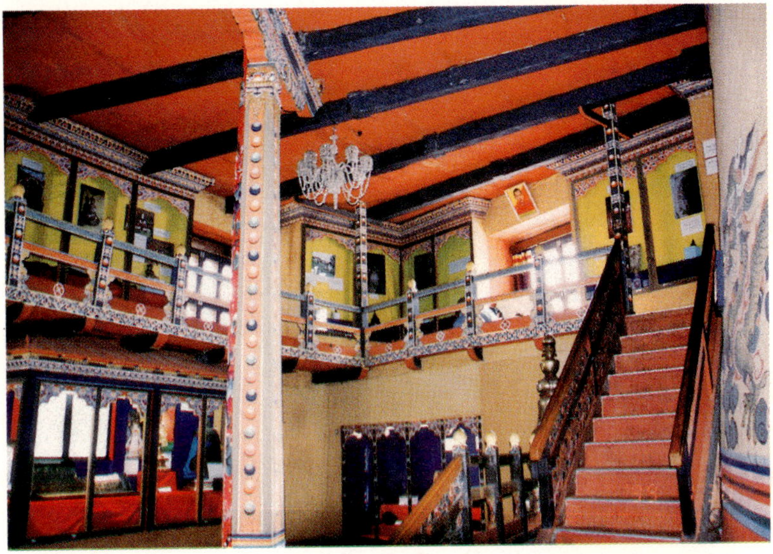

Fourth Floor: 2nd rearranged special exhibition of 1997 on the theme of "Medieval History of Bhutan" covering period from 11 to 15 century AD

Plate # 10

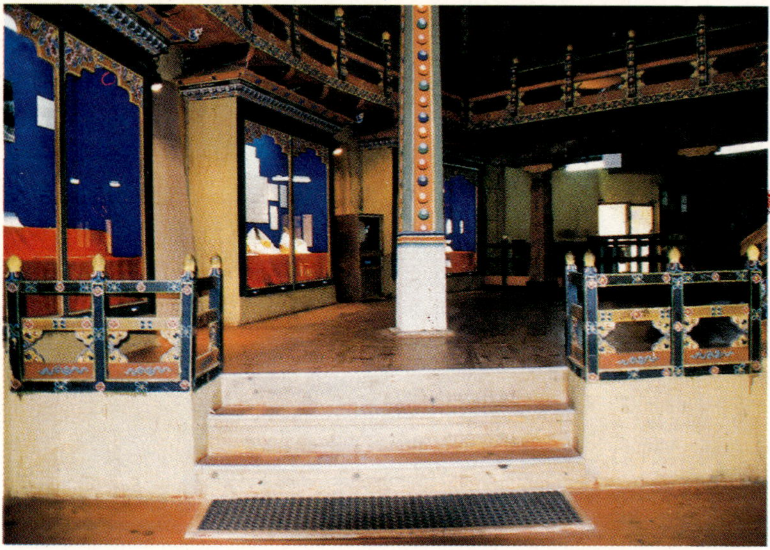

Fourth Floor: 3rd rearranged special exhibition of 1998 on the theme of "Bhutan in the 16th Century".

Plate # 11

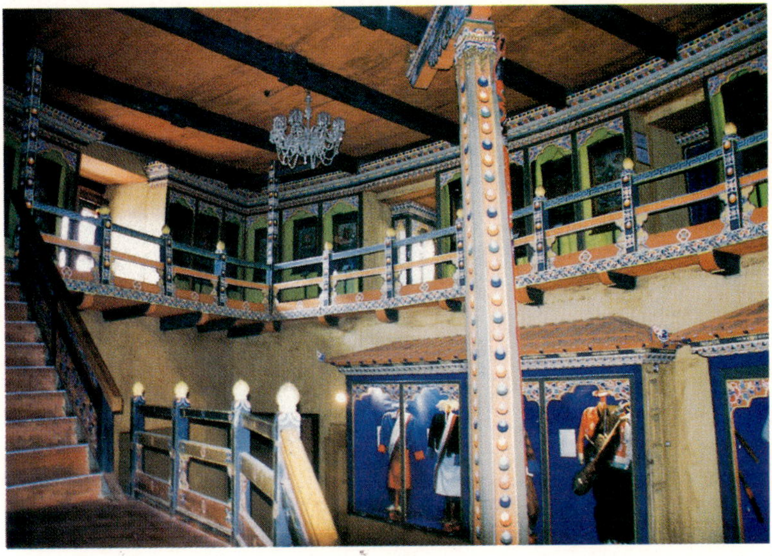

Fourth Floor: 3rd rearranged special exhibition of 1998 on the theme of “Bhutan in the 16th Century”.

Plate # 12

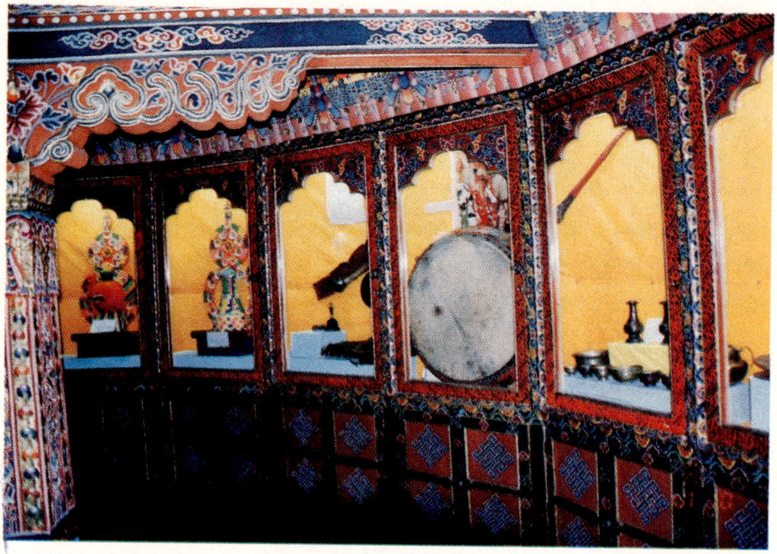

Third Floor: Decorative Arts
Ritual objects, religious musical instruments and Bali (Torma)

Plate # 13

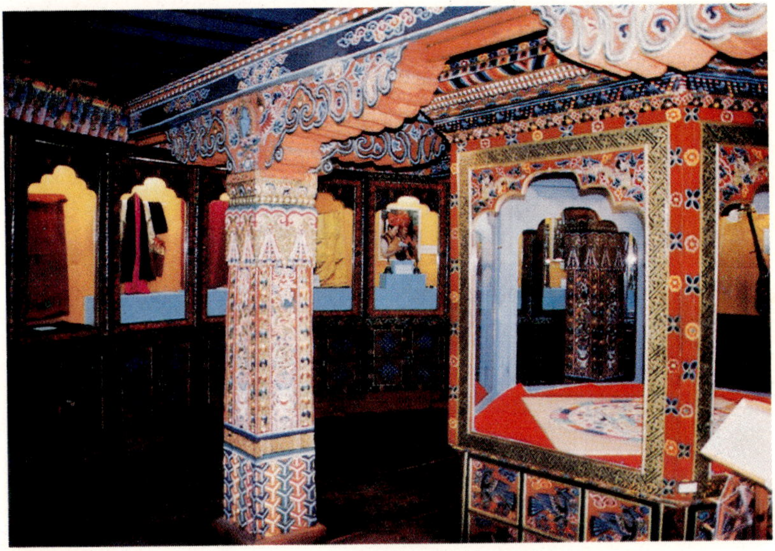

Third Floor: Decorative Arts
Religious costumes
and Mandala

Plate # 14

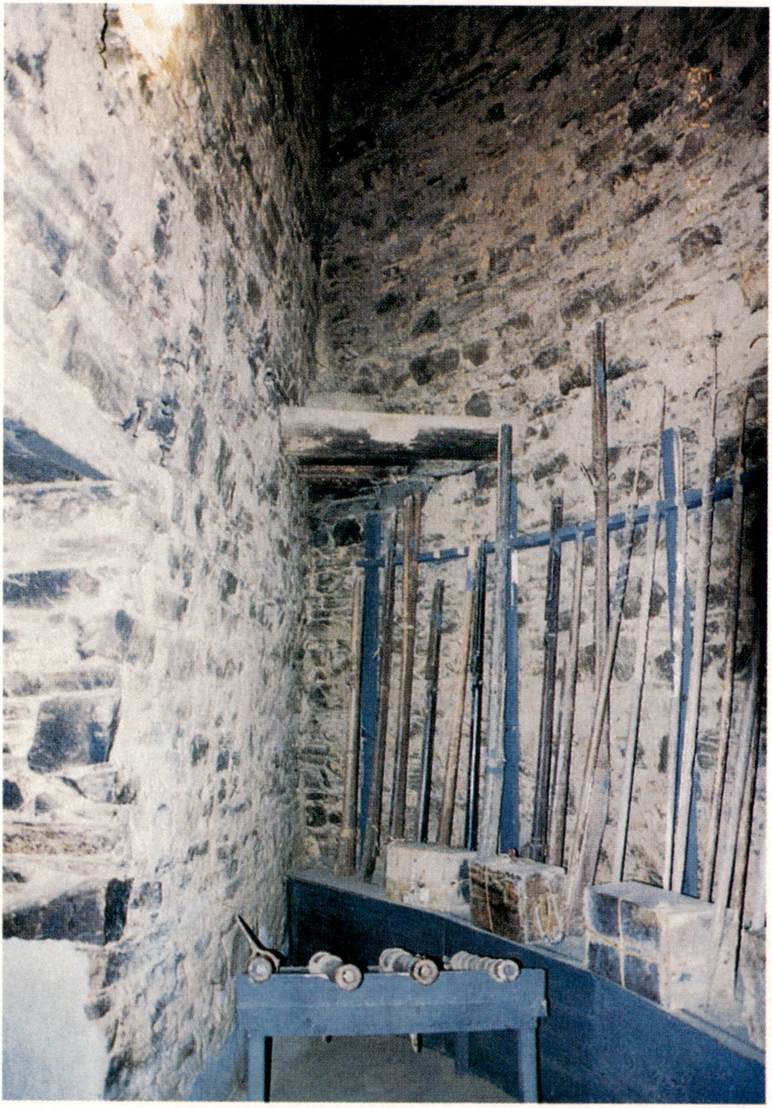

Ground Floor: Ancient arms.

Plate # 15

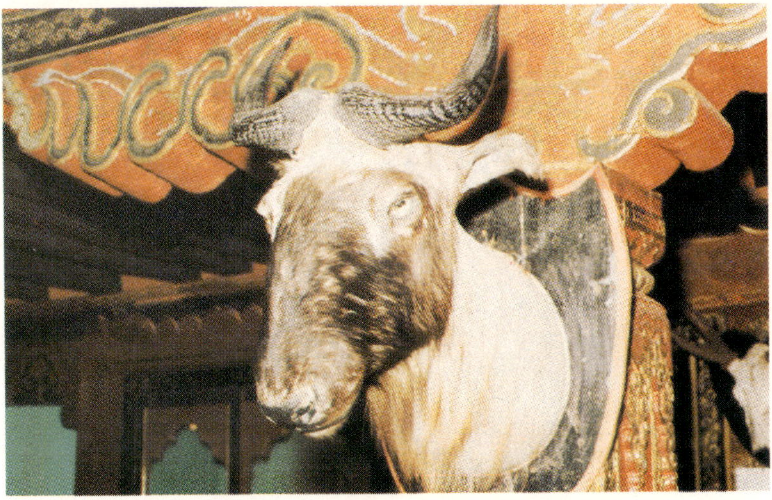

Second Floor: Natural History of Bhutan
Golden Takin, National
animal of Bhutan

Plate # 16

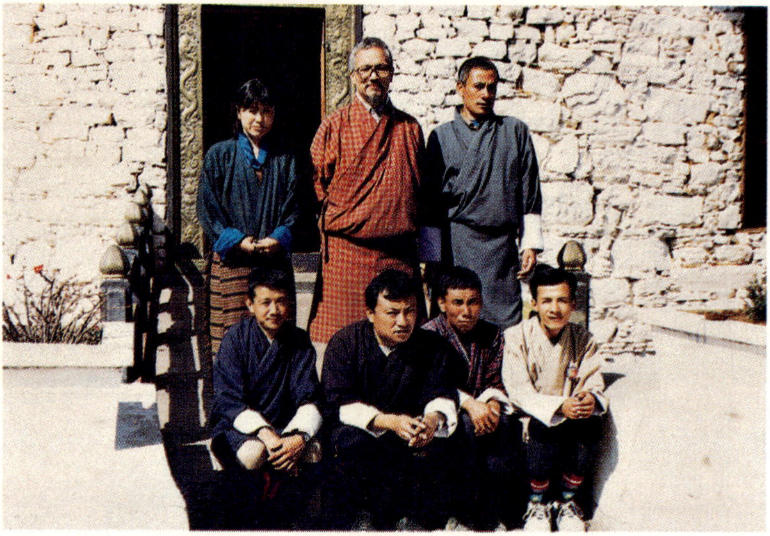

Ta-Dzong Gate: The Author with Museum Staff

XIII CARE AND MAINTENANCE OF ART OBJECTS

There are two trained conservators in the National Museum to take care of the day-to-day care and maintenance of the art objects on display.

Care and maintenance work is not generally considered as conservation work but day-to-day business of getting basic objects cleaning especially before placing them on display. If the condition of an object is very bad then necessary maintenance should be done before moving it from one place to another and before storage. It is a basic preventive conservation work involving specialist object cleaning as well as some minor repairs as and when necessary.

It is necessary to take proper care and maintenance of the collections not only to preserve but also extend their physical integrity by establishing minimum standards of physical care and regular schedules for maintenance. The condition of collections must be monitored and assessed. The conservator, in consultation with the curatorial staff, should decide the schedules for preventive and practical conservation as well as overall conservation strategy and programme for its implementation. All curatorial staff must be well trained to handle the collections in their care. A regular inspection should be done by the curator. In case of a damage occurred, an immediate remedial action should be initiated by the concerned curator.

XIV CONSERVATION

Conservation in broader sense means recording the condition of the objects in the collections or co-ordinating with Conservation Department in conservation of objects. A conservator unit should be established in a Museum for timely conservation. Conservation laboratory should have necessary equipment, accessories and chemicals for conservation work in addition to well qualified and trained conservators. Furthermore, conservation laboratory, design studio, contemporary workshop are necessary in a Museum for research and practical demonstration.

A need for a central conservation and scientific examination laboratory to cater to the needs of the various monasteries, temples, museums and private organizations is felt. Such a laboratory can carry on the chemical treatment and preservation of museum collections and thus preserve the cultural heritage of the country. Various of deterioration and decay lead to irreparable damage or demolition of museum objects, and it has now been accepted that most of the valuable fergile specimens of history and art would have been lost if some kind of chemical treatment had not been given to them for preservation. This work is of a highly specialized nature and needs an uptodate, well equipped laboratory. The requirements are for scientific equipment, a library, a trained staff and space all adequately balanced to maintain a certain standard.

The would be called conservation laboratory of the National Museum should be so fitted and equipped as to be able to undertake the kind of work that comes in the laboratory. In the complete set up the laboratory will have the following sections:

(i) General laboratory
(ii) Research
(iii) Paintings (oil, water colour, panel and frescos)
(iv) Textile

There should be chemists, physicists, artists, photographers, technicians and carpenters who will work for the common cause. A departmental library must be attached to the laboratory, which will have the various books and current journals on the subject available for ready reference. Adequate stores of apparatus, equipment, and chemicals must be built up.

XV STORAGE SYSTEM

The present storage system at the National Museum is very traditional and it needs development and modernization.

In fact, storage is as important as that of the display. Especially textiles are very susceptible to damage from poor physical storage and from incorrect and careless handling and they should not be folded, distorted or insensitively mounted. All these factors combine to pose particular challenges in providing safe storage and accessibility. There are different types of storage systems for textiles which include rolled, flat, boxed or deep drawer, hanging, vertical or sloped and special fittings.

Special attention should be paid to the light, temperature and humidity, dust and pest control for the storage of textiles. The reason being that dyes fade when textiles are exposed to any form of light but ultra-violet light is the most damaging component of light. Temperature and humidity must be monitored in the storage areas.

The insects are fond of hot and humid environment. It is preferable to keep levels towards the lower scale of recommendations to reduce the risk of insect infestation. The insects breed in dark and dirty places. Therefore, avoid open cavities underneath and between storage units. All areas should be regularly cleaned and kept as dust free as possible. Mezzanine walkways should be solid to prevent dirt and dust falling through to the objects storage areas below. All outer clothing including coats should be kept in the cloakroom because people create dust which is unavoidable.

All newly acquired materials should be kept in isolation and sterilized by freezing or some cases fumigation on the ground floor before being taken into storage areas to avoid infestation. It is necessary to carry out a regular inspection of use of pest traps, checking inside drawers and other storage units for signs of infestation at an interval of every six months.

The location of storage is important while planning a museum because staff have to work in the storage areas freely behind secure doors and partitions with easy access to the handling areas when objects have to be moved. The storage space should be large enough to store the textiles with large tables to work on. This should be a secure area with controlled access for the staff to work in this area curating collections. It is necessary to have a room for the storage of materials used in the storage and display textiles with a large table/bench for sewing and other preparation process. In the case of textile, it should be handled very carefully and never with soiled hands. Stains once caused are difficult to remove. It should be ensured that when taken out for study they are kept on clean tables which are covered with cloth. No food or drink, no ink or similar liquid, should be allowed in the storage areas. A special conditioned room for the storage of fur and skin objects and a separate store for the storage of mannequins and display stands used in exhibitions are necessary.

XVI SECURITY MEASURES

It is necessary to ensure that the collections are secure from theft, vandalism, human error, mechanical failure and deterioration. The items must be stored and displayed in prescribed and secure areas. Entry to these areas should be restricted to the relevant curatorial staff. The internal space of the museum should be properly insulated from external conditions. Necessary security measures should be taken against existing and identified threats including fire, flood, vandalism and theft, terrorism and bio-deterioration.

(i) Fire is the most dangerous and serious which coulee destroy the entire site if not brought under control with appropriate defense countermeasures by security personnel in particular and all staff members in general.

(ii) Flood includes rain from the roofs and pipe-burst or likage from below which cause considerable damage to the fabrics and other museum objects. Periodical inspection of the pipelines and surrounding by the security personnel is important. Other staff members should inform the security personnel if they notice any likage of roofs or pipelines.

(iii) Vandalism and theft. There is high risk because of valuable objects in the collections which needs appropriate defense countermeasures by security personnel in particular and all staff in general.

(iv) Terrorism. The terrorism generally prefer soft targets and aim at the museums.

(v) Bio-deterioration is one the major causes of deterioration of cultural property and extensive studies have been done world-wide in the area of bio-deterioration for conservation and preservation of cultural property for the benefit of future generation. Adequate number of conservators should be trained to conserve the objects before deterioration.

The insects are fond of hot and humid environment. It is preferable to keep levels towards the lower scale of recommendations to reduce the risk of insect infestation. The insects breed in dark and dirty places.

The National Museum has taken the following security measures:

(i) Entrusting responsibility of the galleries to the respective Museum Assistants
(ii) Locking systems of all shelves
(iii) 4 Museum Assistants on duty during day time
(iv) 4 Night Guards
(v) CCTV
(vi) Shadow alarm
(vii) No cameras and bags are allowed inside the museum

XVII COLLOQUIA ON BHUTANESE HISTORY AND CULTURE

In conjunction with the re-arranged special exhibitions, the National Museum also conducted three colloquia on Bhutanese history and culture which were attended by Bhutanese scholars.

The 1st colloquium was held on 24 - 25 July 1997 which was attended by the following 11 Bhutanese scholars who presented papers on different aspects of Bhutanese history and culture:

SL. NO.	NAME OF PARTICIPANT	TITLE OF PAPER
1	H. E. Lyonpo (Dr.) Kinzang Dorji	The Role of Astrology in the Local Practice of Bhutanese Farming
2	Dasho Sangay Dorji	Bhutanese Stupa
3	Dasho Sangay Wangchug	Development of Bhutanese Script
4	Lam Choechong	Religious Sash
5	Gonpo Tshering	Bhutanese Songs
6	Lopon Jigme Chhogyel	Bhutan's Culture
7	Dr. C. T. Dorji	Sources of Ancient Bhutanese History
8	Dorji Wangchuk	Conservation of Cultural Properties (Metal Objects)
9	Karma Ura	The Road to Lingzhi
10	Dr. Karma Wangchuk	Pre-historic Bhutan
11	Dr. Yonṭen Dargye	Drukpa Kagyud School
12	Dorji Namgyel	Monuments of Bhutan

The 2nd colloquium was held on 23 - 24 February 1999 which was attended by the following 10 Bhutanese scholars who presented papers on different aspects of Bhutanese history and culture:

SL. NO.	NAME OF PARTICIPANT	TITLE OF PAPER
1	Dasho Sangay Dorji -	Background History of Dungtse Lhakhang
2	Lam Choechong -	Explanation on Dorji Drilbu
3	Lam Dampa Minjur -	A Brief History of Zhabdrung Rinpochhe
4	Khenpo Phuntsok Tashi -	Explanation on Tshokshing Lhakhang
5	Karma Ura -	Bazip Bagi Lim
6	Lopon Jigme Chhogyel-	Neydah-Zhidha
7	Shastri Ugyen Tenzin-	Bhutanese Costumes
8	Dr. Yonten Dargye -	Seal of Nga-Chudug
9	Dr. C. T. Dorji -	Zamling Gyandug Chhognyi
10	Singye Dorji -	Conservation and Protection of Bhutan's Cultural Heritage

The 3rd colloquium was held on 15 -17 January 2001 at Thimphu which was attended by the following 10 Bhutanese scholars who presented papers on significance of Dzongs built by Zhabdrung Ngawang Namgyel in the 17th century AD:

SL. NO.	NAME OF PARTICIPANT		TITLE OF PAPER
1	Dasho Sangay Dorji	-	Paro Dzong
2	Lopon Jigme Chhogyel	-	Punakha Dzong
3	Khenpo Phuntsok Tashi	-	Daga Dzong
4	Dr. Yonten Dargye	-	Wangdi Dzong
5	Lopon Tengay	-	Tashichhodzong
6	Dr. Pema Dorji	-	Introduction to Traditional Medicines
7	Dr. Jagar Dorji	-	Lhop Community
8	Dr. C. T. Dorji	-	The National Museum of Bhutan

In addition to the participants, there were many observers representing different Ministries, Departments and Organizations who also actively participated in the question-answer session which made the colloquia more informative, educative and meaningful. The proceedings too were published funded by the Japan Foundation Asia Center for the same purpose.

The National Museum will continue with the colloquium on different aspects of Bhutanese history and culture in order to do research on these important subjects by Bhutanese scholars. Such research works will highly develop the literature of the history, culture and religion of our country for the benefit of future generation.

The proceedings of these colloquia were published and distributed to the schools and institutions which became an authentic source of reference.

XVIII RESEARCH AND PUBLICATIONS

The National Museum of Bhutan has made a modest beginning in the research area since 1996 and worked on various research activities including the development of appropriate captions and write-ups of the art objects on display at Paro Ta-Dzong Museum as well as preparation of the preliminary draft of Museum Catalogue in two phases i.e. the 1st phase pertaining to 1258 art objects on display at 7 floors of Ta-Dzong Museum and the 2nd phase pertaining to 176 selected art objects lying in the stores at Paro Ta-Dzong. The publication of the Museum Catalogue will also be done shortly.

The research can provide a basic means of guiding the museum into meaningfully functional development. The National Museum should make an attempt to workout a further research policy with good perspectives with a set of sections that covers all of human, natural and inanimate history from the beginning of time and for much of Bhutan in general. It must take account of collections built up over long periods, in some cases over centuries. Research would lead to a transcending traditional bounds and point to an increasingly missionary role in education and in the community. It would contribute substantially to museological studies at practical and theoretical levels also, as part of the infrastructure of museum work within country.

(i) Museum Guidebook
(ii) Museum Catalogue
(iii) Proceedings of Colloquia
(iv) Leaf-lets and brochures

Realizing the need and importance of a Museum Catalogue, the National Museum engaged the Joint Director who prepared the preliminary draft of the Museum Catalogue and submitted to Hon'ble Chairman, National Commission for Cultural Affairs in 2 phases as follows:

(i) 1st Phase: The preliminary draft of Museum Catalogue pertaining to 1258 art objects on display at 7 floors of Ta-Dzong Museum

(ii) 2nd Phase: The preliminary draft of Museum Catalogue pertaining to 176 selected art objects lying in the stores at Paro Ta-Dzong

The National Museum proposes to publish Museum Catalogue with a selected and master pieces of artifacts during the 9FYP which will become a major research work on the art objects on display at the National Museum, Paro Ta-Dzong.

The proceedings of three colloquia on Bhutanese history and culture and Dzongs of Bhutan were published financed by the Japan Foundation

Asia Center and distributed to the schools and institutions throughout the country which became not only permanent documents but also most authentic source of information on our rich history and culture. These publications could be used by the research scholars as valuable source of reference in the near future.

The continuation of conducting colloquia on different aspects of Bhutanese history and culture and publication of the proceedings during the 9FYP will certainly develop Bhutanese literature both in Dzongkha and English for the benefit of not only Bhutanese students but also for the research fellows as valuable reference in the near future. Therefore, the National Museum proposes to continue the colloquia and publication of the proceedings as core activities.

XIX MUSEUM EDUCATION PROGRAMME

In Bhutan, the Museum Education Programme is a new concept and approach to provide education to the students as well adults. This comes under non-formal education but it is very effective to learn through three dimensional visual objects. The museum education programme includes school visits, gallery talks, gallery sheets, worksheets for students, sketching, drawing competition, clay modeling and special lectures. The museum education programme would integrate museum into a class-room besides their theoretical learning in the school.

In this regard, ever since a Joint Director was transferred from the Royal Institute of Management, Thimphu to the National Museum, Paro, a modest beginning has been made to give Gallery Talk and lectures on different aspects of Bhutanese history and culture to the organized group of tourists and students visiting the museum. Bhutanese students from high schools, junior high schools, primary schools and training institutes started visiting the National Museum every year as part of their study programmes. This has resulted in popularizing the National Museum as the following tables of last 5 years (1996-2000) will depict a clear position of the students who visited the National Museum, Paro Ta-Dzong.

STATEMENT OF BHUTANESE STUDENTS WHO VISITED THE NATIONAL MUSEUM, PARO TA-DZONG FROM 1996 TO 2000

Year		Number of Students	No. Teachers
1996	-	72	4
1997	-	120	6
1998	-	200	9
1999	-	334	15
2000	-	903	25
	Total	1629	59

Now the National Museum will be in a better position to enhance the Gallery Talk and lectures on Bhutanese history and culture since the Assistant Curator has come back from the National Museum Institute, New Delhi with an M. A. in Museology who can assist the Joint Director. Therefore, it is necessary to introduce the Museum Education Programme in the National Museum as a core activity of the museum.

XX HRD AND TRAINING

Keeping in view of the importance of Human Resource Development, the National Museum developed the staff by imparting necessary training in relevant fields like museology and conservation to the following officials and staff during the 8FYP:

(i) Dorji Wangchuk, Lab. Asstt. attended 6 months course on Museum Management at Osaka sponsored by the JICA

(ii) Dorji Namgyel, Assistant Curator attended 6 months course on Conservation in NRLC, Lucknow

(iii) Dorji Namgyel, Assistant Curator attended 2 and half years M.A. in Museology in the National Museum Institute, New Delhi

(iv) Dr. C. T. Dorji, Joint Director attended a short course on "Care and Maintenance of Art Objects" in NRLC, Lucknow and a short attachment course on "Carbon Dating (14 C)" at BSIP, Lucknow

(v) Dr. C. T. Dorji, Joint Director attended a short course on lacquer works at Tokyo

(vi) Dr. C. T. Dorji, Joint Director was awarded UK Visiting Fellowship by the Nehru Trust in 1999-2000 and he visited many museums, art galleries and conservation centers in the UK. As a part of his fellowship programme, Dr. Dorji prepared a comprehensive report on "Management of Textile Museum"

(vii) Gem Tshering, Conservator attended 6 months course on Conservation at the NRLC, Lucknow

(viii) Gem Tshering, Conservator attended one week seminar on Conservation of Paintings in the TNRTI, Tokyo

(ix) Deki Yangzom, Office Secretary attended 6 months course on Museum Management in Osaka sponsored by the JICA

In order to continue with the Human Resource Development, the National Museum proposes the following training programme for the staff during the 9FYP which will also enable the staff to discharge their job responsibilities more effectively and efficiently:

(i) Long-term course in Museology, Archaeology, Art History and Conservation

(ii) Short-term course on Museology, Archaeology, Art History and Conservation

(iii) Short-term course in Computer at AIT, Bangkok

(iv) Short-term course in Research Methodology and Publications

(v) Attend Workshops, Seminars and Conferences on museology, archaeology, conservation, art history and other related subjects

XXI BENEFIT OF THE NATIONAL MUSEUM FOR BHUTANESE STUDENTS

The concept of museum has changed from that of a ware-house of antiquities to an educational institution of cultural heritage, history, arts, science, design etc. The concept is further strengthened and developed worldwide by introduction of "museum education programme" and "mobile museum exhibition" which have been incorporated in the various activities of a museum. Every museum is now equipped with guide lecturers who are not only qualified in the subjects like history, culture, archaeology, art history and museology but also well trained to guide the visitors and give gallery talks. Now the museum is a center of learning through visual display of the objects which attract many visitors, teachers, students and research scholars. It is easily comprehended and retained in the minds when something is learnt through visual display as compared to reading books and listening to the classroom lectures. The young mind should be saturated with the idea that it has been born in a human world which is in harmony with the world around it.

In accordance with the new concept of museum as an educational institution of cultural heritage, history, arts, science, design etc., the National Museum of Bhutan also made a modest beginning to invite the students and teachers from different parts of the country to see the display of art objects and attend gallery talks on Bhutanese history and culture and art objects on permanent display at Paro Ta-Dzong. The National Museum of Bhutan has become quite popular especially after the introduction of re-arranged special exhibitions beginning 1996 and gallery talks as the number of students and teachers keeps on increasing steadily year by year.

TABLE OF BHUTANESE STUDENTS WHO VISITED THE NATIONAL MUSEUM OF BHUTAN DURING LAST 5 YEARS (1996-2000)

Year		Number of Students	No. Teachers
1996	-	72	4
1997	-	120	6
1998	-	200	9
1999	-	334	15
2000	-	903	25
Total		1629	59

TABLE OF BHUTANESE STUDENTS WHO VISITED THE NATIONAL MUSEUM OF BHUTAN DURING 1999

Sl. No.	Name of School	No. of Students	No. of Teachers
1	Shaba School, Paro	112	2
2	PTC, Paro	98	4
3	Paro Jr. High School	3	
5	Lango Pry. School, Paro	90	3
5	School of Arts & Crafts, Thimphu	31	3
	Total	334	12

TABLE OF BHUTANESE STUDENTS WHO VISITED THE NATIONAL MUSEUM OF BHUTAN DURING 2000

Sl. No.	Name of School	No. of Students	No. of Teacher
1	Rinpung Pry. School, Paro	130	6
2	Bhutan Forest Institute, Taba, Thimphu	36	2
3	Paro Jr. High School	523	6
4	Drugyel High School, Paro	25	1
5	Shaba High School, Paro	75	1
6	Institute of Language & Cultural Studies, Simtokha, Thimphu	23	2
7	Samtse Jr. High School	16	2
8	NIE, Paro	27	1
	Sub-Total	855	24
9	RBP Training Centre, Gelephu	48	1
	Grand Total	903	25

TABLE OF INDIAN STUDENTS WHO VISITED THE NATIONAL MUSEUM OF BHUTAN DURING 2000

Sl. No.	Name of School	No. of Students	No. of Teachers
1	Sarvajana Naidu Govt. Girls' College, Bhopal	78	9
2	Mahadevi Birla Girls' Higher Secondary School, Calcutta	70	5
3	St. Thomas' Boys' School, Calcutta	16	5
4	Robert Money Technical High School & Jr. College, Bombay	47	3
5	Visvabharati, Santiniketan	9	2
	Total	220	24

As Bhutanese, it is vitally important to know not only about the history and culture of our country but also the historical perspective of 4 major schools of Mahayana Buddhism in general and Kagyu tradition in particular a brief account of the following chief Kagyu Lamas:

- Vajradhara *(RDOR-JE HCHANG),*
- Tilopa (988-1069),
- Naropa (1016-1100),
- Marpa (1012-1097),
- Mila (1040-1123),
- Gampopa alias Dagpo Lhaje (1079-1153),
- Thatsapa alias Phagmo Duba Dorji (1110-1153),
- Naphupa alias Lingray Padma (1128-1198),
- Palden Drukpa alias Drogon Tsangpa Gyarey Yeshey Dorji (1161-1211).

The students can learn through visual display of the statues, thangkas and other art objects. Among others, the students can have a glimpse of the following important personalities in a few hours in the museum:

1 **Tshogshing Lhakhang: The Temple of Tree of Wisdom or Field of Buddhas, the *sui genres* of Bhutan, explains the entire history of Mahayana Buddhism and it's propagation. There are four**

major schools of Mahayana Buddhism i.e. Nyingma, Sakya, Gelug and Kagyu. Each major school of Mahayana Buddhism has its own Tshogshing to explain the history and hierarchy or levels of the masters but the Tshogshing at Paro Ta-Dzong built in 1968 is non-sectarian. As such, it has masters from all major schools of Mahayana Buddhism e.g. On the eastern side, there is Vajradhara *(RDOR-JE HCHANG)* in the center top with Tilopa and Naropa of India and Marpa and Milarepa of Kagyupa lineage. Some of the main Tantric deities such as Chakrasamvara *(HKHOR-LO SDOM-PA)*, Hevajra *(KYE-RDOR-JE)*, Kalachakra *(DUS-HKHOR)*, Guhyasamaj *(GSANG-BA HDUS-PA)*, three goddesses and three protective deities are shown on the east side. The main images are Dagpo Lhaje on the southern side, Guru Padmasambhava on the western side while Atisha Dipankara Srijana *(Jowo Je Palden Atisha)* on the northern side. There are three main purposes of having Tshogshing Lhakhang in top floor of the National Museum of Bhutan at Paro Ta-Dzong which are:

- **It is a place of worship**
- **The students of Buddhist Studies can understand the iconography better**
- **The meditators can visualize the hierarchy and level of their masters**

2 The Sixteen Arhats *(GNAS-BRTAN BCHU-DRUG)* are of great importance in Bhutanese Buddhism. It is said that for the welfare of the Sangha, Buddha selected sixteen Arhats from his disciples and entrusted them with the duty of preserving, protecting and propagating the Dharma. Normally sixteen Arhats are shown with four guardian deities of four directions and Dharmatala and Hva-Sang.

3 Zamling Gyandrug Chhognyi or The Six Ornaments and Two Most Excellent Ones: Nagarjuna *(KLU-SGRUB)* and Asanga *(THOGS-MED)* are traditionally known as the Two Most Excellent Ones while Arya Deva *(HPHAGS-PA-LHA)*, Vasubandu *(DBYIG-GNYEN)*, Dignaga *(PHYOGS-GLANG)*, Dharmakirti *(CHHOS-GRAGS)*, Gurnaprabha *(YONTEN-HOD)* and Shakyaprabha *(SHAH-KYA-HOD)* are known as the six Ornaments of the Buddhist world. However, in some Indian traditions they refer to Gurnaprabha and Shakyaprabha as the Two Most Excellent Ones. The writings by these Eight Great scholars are found in Tenjur (commentarial canon) and are accepted by all sects of Mahayana Buddhism and quotation on any point is accepted by all.

(i) Nagarjuna *(KLU-SGRUB)* is one of the Six Ornaments of the Buddhist World *(RGYAN-DRUG)*. Born at Vidharba in South India during 1-2 century

AD. The books authored by him are found in Tenjur and are accepted by all sects of Mahayana Buddhism and any quotation on any point is accepted by all.

(ii) Asanga *(THOGS-MED)* is one of the Six Ornaments of the Buddhist World *(RGYAN-DRUG)*. Born at Purushapura (Peshawar) in Pakistan in 3rd century AD. The books authored by him are found in Tenjur and are accepted by all sects of Mahayana Buddhism and any quotation on any point is accepted by all.

(iii) Arya Deva *(HPHAGS-PA-LHA)* is one of the Six Ornaments of the Buddhist World *(RGYAN-DRUG)*. Born in Simhala present Sri Lanka in 2nd century AD. The books authored by him are found in Tenjur and are accepted by all sects of Mahayana Buddhism and any quotation on any point is accepted by all.

(iv) Dharmakirti *(CHHOS-GRAGS)* is one of the Six Ornaments of the Buddhist World *(RGYAN-DRUG)*. Born in Tirumalla (Tirmala) in Chola country i.e. North Tamil Nadu, India in 7th century AD. The books authored by him are found in Tenjur and are accepted by all sects of Mahayana Buddhism and any quotation on any point is accepted by all.

(v) Vasubandhu *(DBYIG-GNYEN)* is one of the Six Ornaments of the Buddhist World *(RGYAN-DRUG)*. Born at Purushapura (Peshawar) in Pakistan in 3rd century AD. He was younger brother of Asanga (Thogmed). The books authored by him are found in Tenjur and are accepted by all sects of Mahayana Buddhism and any quotation on any point is accepted by all.

(vi) Dignaga *(PHYOGS-GLANG)* is one of the Six Ornaments of the Buddhist World *(RGYAN-DRUG)*. Born in Sinhavatara near Kanchi (Kanchipuram) in South India in 4-5 century AD. The books authored by him are found in Tenjur and are accepted by all sects of Mahayana Buddhism and any quotation on any point is accepted by all.

(vii) Gunaprabha *(YONTEN-HOD)* is one of the Two Most Excellent Ones of the Buddhist World *(MCHOG-GNYIS)*. Born at Mathura in India in 7 century AD. The books authored by him are found in Tenjur and are accepted by all sects of Mahayana Buddhism and any quotation on any point is accepted by all.

(viii) Shakyaprabha *(SHAH-KYA-HOD)* is one of the Two Most Excellent Ones the Buddhist World *(MCHOG-GNYIS)*. Born in Western India in 8 century AD during the reign of Gopala, the father of King Dharmapala who built Vikramasila monastery in

India. The books authored by him are found in Tenjur and are accepted by all sects of Mahayana Buddhism and any quotation on any point is accepted by all.

The set of Gyen-drug Chhog-nyi Thangkas on display at the National Museum, Paro Ta-Dzong is a unique one because it shows Shariputra and Mahamogalayan as Two Most Excellent Ones. This must be a mistake by the painter who wrote the names of each saint with golden letters under the portrait.

4 Guru Padma Jungney is normally depicted with 8 Manifestations *(GURU-MTSHEN-BRGYAD)* and his two consorts Lhacham Mendarawa (Princess of Mandi, Himachal Pradesh, India) and Khandu Yeshey Tshogyel (Queen of Tibet). Guru Padma Jungney, better known as Ugyen Guru Rinpochhey is an Indian Saint of the 8th century. Considered as the second Buddha who introduced Tantric Buddhism in the Himalayan countries including Tibet and Bhutan. He is revered by all traditions of Mahayana Buddhism. In Bhutan there are many places associated with him including Kurje in Bumthang, Gyon Tshephug in Gasa and Taktshang in Paro.

5 Marpa Chhoekyi Lodroe (1012-1097) was one of the chief Kagyu Lamas as well as a great translator (lotsawa). He was the main disciple of a renowned Indian saint, Naropa (1016-1100). Marpa translated many Buddhist texts from Indian languages into Chhoekey (classical language) including those Tantric texts on Guhyasamaja *(GSANG-WA HDUS-PA)* and Chakrasamvara *(HKHOR-LO-SDOM-PA)*. He passed on his teachings to Jetsun Milarepa.

6 Jetsun Milarepa (1040-1123) was also one of the chief Kagyu Lamas. He was disciple of Marpa Chhoekyi Lodroe and was a great poet. He attained full enlightenment in a single life-time. Therefore, he is often taken as an example for perseverance and determination for the quest of learning and spiritual accomplishment. He was very famous for composition of poems and songs which are still used for reference. He passed on his teachings to Gampopa (1079-1153) and Rechungpa (1084-1161). The four major and eight minor schools of Kagyu were introduced by the disciples of these two great masters. Drukpa Kagyu is the State Religion of Bhutan introduced by Lama Phajo Drugom Zhigpo in 1220 AD.

7 Phajo Drugom Zhigpo (1208-1276) arrived in Bhutan in 1220 AD.

8 Dupthob Thangtong Gyalpo, popularly known as Lama Chazampa (1385-1464) was one of the five groups of Lamas *(Lam-Kha-Nga).* He entered Bhutan in 1433 and played a vital role in political affairs in Bhutan.

9 Terton Padma Lingpa (1450-1521) was a great 15th century Nyingmapa saint who discovered many valuable and sacred treasures *(GTER)* in Bhutan mainly in Bumthang valley.

10 Drukpa Kunley, the "Divine Mad Man" (1455-1529) arrived in western Bhutan in the 15th century. He became without doubt, the most popular man of religion in Bhutan.

11 Zhabdrung Ngawang Namgyal (1594-1651).

12 The students can also learn about the lives and deeds of Druk Desis and Je Khenpos.

13 The students can also learn about the contributions made by four hereditary monarchs for the socio-economic development of Bhutan.

14 In addition to the above, the students can learn about the following artifacts:

- philately of Bhutan
- dzongs and monasteries
- ancient arms, ammunitions and armours
- decorative arts including bronze, copper, silver, earthen tea pots and other utensils
- jewelry and costumes
- religious artifacts, religious objects and religious costumes
- natural history including wild animals, birds, reptiles and butterflies
- lacquer-ware and wooden utensils of daily use
- bamboo and cane products of daily use
- urns of different metals and other utensils used in the olden days

15 Bhutanese way of life through different stages of socio-economic development

XXII VISITOR SERVICES

As far as the visitor services are concerned, so far, there is only one public toilet to cater to the general visitors and a cafeteria for the VVIP's and government guests at Paro Ta-Dzong.

However, it is understood that the idea of visitor services is to bring together a number of disparate functions into something more cohesive in order to deliver qualitative services to the visitors. This is a co-ordinating unit for efficient and effective functioning of a museum. The customer care or making provision of positive, effective and friendly hosting to every visitor to the Museum is important. Any visitor who leaves the museum disappointed with the guidance, help or manner should be viewed as a potential failure on the part of the museum management requiring review of the procedure and performance which warrant corrective measures. The visitors are unlikely to return to the museum after a bad experience nor tell their friends to visit the museum. It is important to note that the visitors' perception matters, not that of the museum management. Providing the highest standard of customer care to visitors is essential. It is important that all areas should be accessible to visitors with disabilities and consideration of their needs should be taken into account when planning visible storage and use of other public areas.

As a matter of fact, visitor services include cleaning, catering, reception and information desk, waiting room with smoking area, cloakroom, souvenir shop, restaurant, lavatories, retiring room for museum staff and car-parking. It is also a revenue generating unit not only through admission fees but also through a greater spend by the visitors in the shops and restaurant.

XXIII GENERAL INFORMATION

Opening Time:
Sunday : 11.00 AM - 4.00 PM
Mondays & National Holidays: Closed
Tuesday - Saturday : 09.00 AM - 4.00 PM

Admission Fee:
Locals : Nu. 5.00
SAARC member countries : Nu. 50.00
Foreign Tourists : Nu. 100.00
Children are free

Visitors are requested to refrain from the following:

1 To touch or copy any piece on display
2 Smoking inside the Museum
3 No bags, cameras and video cameras are allowed inside the Museum
4 Photography is possible only with special permission

NATIONAL MUSEUM OF BHUTAN
TA-DZONG
PO PARO, BHUTAN

Telephone No. 975-8-271470/271511/271257
Fax. No. 975-8-271510
E-mail: nmb@druknet.net.bt

XXIV CONCLUSION

The Museum as an educational institution of cultural heritage, history, arts, science, design etc. plays a vital role not only for school education but also for public education. Neither books nor lectures can bring vividly before us the understanding of the past glory whereas in a museum, history is revealed before us in stone and colour. The concept of museum is further strengthened and developed worldwide by introduction of "museum education programme" and mobile museum exhibition" which have been incorporated in the various activities of a museum. Every museum is now equipped with guide lecturers who are not only qualified in the subjects like history, culture, archaeology, art history and museology but also well trained to guide the visitors and give gallery talks. Now the museum is a center of learning through visual display of the objects which attract many visitors, teachers, students and research scholars. It is easily comprehended and retained in the minds when something is learnt through visual display as compared to reading books and listening to the classroom lectures. The young mind should be saturated with the idea that it has been born in a human world which is in the harmony with the world around it.

Considering the need to expand the museum, the National Museum proposed during the 8FYP to construct a new building with permanent exhibition hall for natural History of Bhutan, auditorium, library, temporary exhibition hall and storage of art objects including audio-visual equipment with modern facilities but it was not approved. As such, we would like to propose the same project again for re-consideration in the 9FYP because the National Museum should have a permanent hall to conduct temporary exhibitions from time to time in addition to house permanent exhibition of natural history of Bhutan, auditorium, library and storage of art objects including Audio-Visual equipment with modern facilities. The Ta-Dzong building being an ancient structure does not have a room for extension to accommodate the above facilities as the National Museum of Bhutan. Therefore, it is necessary to have a new building with modern technology.

The National Museum has, so far, mounted 5 re-arranged special exhibitions from 1996 to 2000 which covered the period from the pre-7th Century to the 17th Century. The 6th re-arranged special exhibition entitled "Desi Era" focused on the 18th and 19th century will be opened on 26 May 2001. The National Museum has been receiving annually Nu. 0.5 m from the Department of Budget and Accounts, Ministry of Finance for the re-arranged special exhibitions.

During the 9th Five Year Plan, the National Museum proposes to establish a Mobile Museum Exhibition. The Mobile Museum Exhibition fitted on a Van could take the museum to the door steps of schools situated in the remote areas of Bhutan. This exhibition can also benefit the villagers who cannot visit the National Museum of Bhutan at Paro Ta-Dzong instead the museum could go to the door steps of the people. At the same time, the Mobile Museum Exhibition is a new approach in popularizing the museum and very powerful means to educate the students and villagers.

Finally, it may not be out of place to state here that conservation and preservation of cultural property is important for the future generation but on the contrary, the control of mind-degradation of cultural value is more important to appreciate the value of cultural heritage so conserved and preserved in the museums. Mind-degradation study is as important as that of biodeterioration study. There is an inevitable need to begin study on mind-degradation of cultural value for the benefit of younger generation. Things embedded in the minds of young children will have a greater impact on their lives and remains permanent impression through their lives. Therefore, we must inculcate moral lessons in the minds of young Bhutanese students for appreciation of cultural value preserved and conserved by our forefathers. One best way of realizing this goal is to recognize the importance of "museum education programme" and the students should visit the museums to see the real world experience in order to produce good citizens dedicated to the cause of the Tsa-Wa-Sum.

REFERENCES:

1 Central Statistical Organization, Planning Commission: Bhutan at a Glance, Thimphu (1999)

2 Dorji, CT: A Brief Account of the National Museum of Bhutan, Paro Ta-Dzong (1998)

3 - History of Bhutan based on Buddhism, New Delhi, Prominent Publishers (1994)

4 - Blue Annals of Bhutan, New Delhi, Vikas Publishers (1997)

5 - Advent and Development of Drukpa Kagyudpa Sect of Buddhism in Bhutan, Conference Paper (1990)

6 - An Introduction to Bhutanese Literature (In Press)

7 - Management of Textile Museum, Victoria & Albert Museum, London (2000)

8 - Importance of the National Museum for Bhutanese Students, Conference paper (2001)

9 - The draft of "Museum Catalogue" (Phase I) pertaining to 1258 art objects on display in the National Museum at Paro Ta-Dzong from October 1996 to June 1998 as per the order of H. E. Lyonpo Dago Tshering, former Home Minister and Chairman of Special Commission for Cultural Affairs

10 - The draft of "Museum Catalogue" (Phase II) pertaining to the art objects lying in the museum stores at Paro Ta-Dzong from December 1998 to April 1999 as per the order of H. E. Lyonpo Thinley Gyamtsho, Hon'ble Home Minister and Chairman of Special Commission for Cultural Affairs

11 - The Concept Paper on Mind-Degradation of Cultural Value and Its Control (1999)

12 Dorji, Rigzin: A Brief Historical Background of the Religious Institutions of Bhutan, Thimphu, Council of Ecclesiastical Affairs (1993)

13 Kuensel: Bhutan's National Newspaper, Thimphu

14 National Museum of Bhutan: Museum Guidebook (1997)

15 Namgyel, D: A Seminar on History of Development of Museums in Bhutan, New Delhi (2000)

16 Nado, Lopon: Druk Karpo (Religious and Political History of Bhutan), Bumthang, Tharpaling Monastery (1986)

17 Rinchhen, Gedhun: Lhoyi Chhoejung Losar Nawi Gyen (Religious History of Bhutan), Zhung Dratshang, Thimphu/Punakha (1990)

Photo plates :

	Ta-Dzong Building (jacket cover)
1	Tshogshing Lhakhang (eastern side)
2	Tshogshing Lhakhang (western side)
3	Tshogshing Lhakhang (southern side)
4	Tshogshing Lhakhang (northern side)
5	Gallery of antique statues
6	Gallery of Thangka paintings
7	Gallery of 1st special exhibition on down and early history of Bhutan
8	Gallery of 1st special exhibition on down and early history of Bhutan
9	Gallery of 2nd special exhibition on medieval history of Bhutan
10	Gallery of 3rd special exhibition on 16 century
11	Gallery of 3rd special exhibition on 16th century
12	Gallery of decorative arts of Bhutan
13	Gallery of decorative arts of Bhutan
14	Gallery of ancient arms of Bhutan
15	Gallery of natural history of Bhutan (Golden Takin, the national animal of Bhutan)
16	Group photograph of the author with museum staff

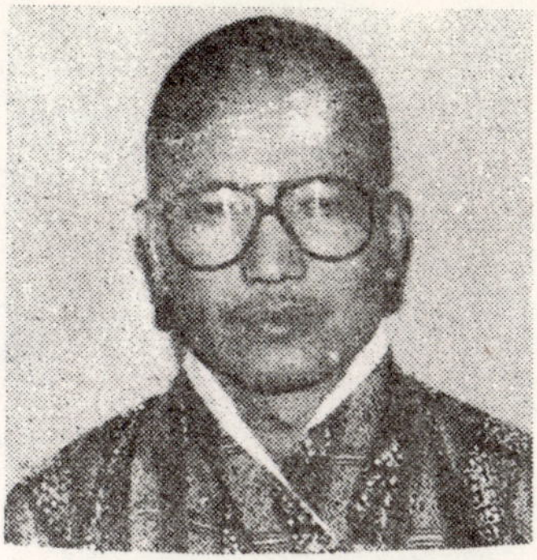

The Author

Dr. C.T. Dorji, Ph.D. (Magadh), M.A. (Double), B.Com., P.G. Dip-in-Public Administration (LSE, London) is civil servant, academic, historian, connoisseur, writer and multi-disciplinary scholar.

He joined Bhutan Civil Service in 1968 and served in various positions. He participated in many international conferences and presented papers on varied subjects. He authored ten books in Bhutanese history and culture and edited and compiled three books on Buddhist Moral Lessons.

He is honoured to be Fellow, Royal Historical Society, London; Deputy Governor, The American Biographical Institute, North Carolina, USA for Bhutan; Member, Research Board of Advisors, The American Biographical Institute, North Carolina, USA; Deputy Director General, The International Biographical Centre, Cambridge, England for Bhutan; Member, Advisory Council, The International Biographical Centre, Cambridge, England; Member, The World Buddhist University Council, Bangkok, Thailand; Regional Editor of WFB Newsletter, The World Fellowship of Buddhist, Bangkok; Member, The International Network of Engaged Buddhists, Bangkok.

Presently, Dr. C.T. Dorji is Joint Director, National Museum of Bhutan, Ta-Dzong, Paro, Bhutan.